MEAT HEART

MEAT HEART

MELISSA BRODER

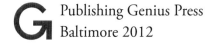
Publishing Genius Press
Baltimore 2012

Publishing Genius Press
1818 East Lafayette Avenue
Baltimore, MD 21213

www.PublishingGenius.com
www.MeatHeart.com

ISBN 13: 978-0-9831706-6-2
Copyright © Melissa Broder 2012

Creative Commons license:
Attribution-NonCommercial-ShareAlike

Cover design by Dress Code
www.DressCodeNY.com
Page design by Adam Robinson

Go, go, go, said the bird: human kind
Cannot bear very much reality.
   T.S. Eliot

ONE

Meat Heart	1
The Mail	2
Bones	3
Championship	4
Pennsylvania Prayer	5
Supper	6
Portrait of My Mother as a Gold Dust Woman	8
Obituary	9
Umbrella Poem	10
Superdoom	12
Such Beautiful Clothes	13
Leah	14
Binge Eating in 2067	16
Ginger	18
Flora	19
Ahoy!	20

TWO

Lonesome Cowgirl	23
Mikveh	24
Ciao Manhattan	26
De Forest Station	28
Flurry	30
Waterfall	31
Megachurch	32
Mercy	34
Puff	35
Mamala	36
Steak Night	38
Prayer of the Restless Caretaker	40
Arson Wife	41
Jacob's Ladder	42
Ringo	43
Ego Deaths of a Queen	44
Early 90s Prayer	46
How to Unline a Journal	47
Blue Period	48
Raise Your Hand If You're Sure	50
Concentrate	51
Facsimile	52
Good Housekeeping	53
Nitrous Oxide	54
Gold Lipstick and the End of Summer	55

THREE

Laissez Fanfic	57
Fugazi Shame	58
Seventh Grade Light Brigade	60
Lack	61
Gate 27	62
30th Edition	64
Sharon Tate, Man Up	66
When Envy Went to Die	68
Drive-In	69
Vertigo	70
African Priestess, Columbus Circle	72
Harriet	73
Hydroponics	74
Bye	76
Today I Will Be a Benevolent Narrator	77
H1N1	78
Mr. Bubble	80
Pink Keds	81
No Hostages	82
Beach House	84
Money Honey	85
Fauna	86
It Is Good	88
Acknowledgments	90

ONE

MEAT HEART

Listen wormhead
There is no celery emergency
No rutabaga for alarm
No evil peach in your vein of air
Or pomegranate on high alert
Though kiwi seeds may streak the soil
And tubers crop up bruised
And cornhusk filaments
Still jacket tongues
There is only Slim Jim love
And taco glow
And all-night burger magic

THE MAIL

I am disgusted by the U.S. mail
its endless soul-crush pulp of catalogs,
utility bills, act now offers and sales
stinking with aggravation.

Just once I would like to reach in the slot
and come upon a stony hollow
or perhaps a tiny garden,
a plot filled with pint-sized animals:

token birds, a little hairless cat
and a mountain range behind it,
a small wall of shadow
to gaze at as I loaf the evening

on a petite porch, a bit of loaf,
cubed cheese, an apple from my tiny tree,
nothing major just a light supper
on chippy, earthenware dishes.

This will be the depth of my story,
the stunning extent of my smile:
a scattered few pinprick dung drops,
some night weather, no envelopes.

BONES

I held a nightlight
to my bones.

Run run said the moon
or build yourself
a rowboat with a roof.

I am like a sailor
who is terrified of fish

if I see a skeleton
I might begin

to vomit up
the mystery
and then what?

I am nothing
like a sailor.

CHAMPIONSHIP

God keeps unfurling me
with god's gigantic helium.
There are scratchmarks all over
my life.   That's from my mitts.
Other human,   this unfurliness
is far too spacious.   Would you
lend me some muscle?   Let's
write a sermon on control. Let's
write a love song for heavyweights
and by heavyweights
I mean everyone.

PENNSYLVANIA PRAYER

Bless me I was once myself and couldn't read
a thermostat. My mother's breasts were long

inside her bathrobe. (Sometimes we were Polish.)
I believe god knows these things about me

so I needn't say them with heart. I'm afraid
to say anything with heart. One summer

there came an ice storm and a skinny lady
flew inside my ear. She forced me to eat

grapes, only grapes, until I wasn't
myself anymore. Wine made me feel myself.

Wine made me somebody else. God knows
there is more to this story. My heart fell out.

SUPPER

Boy comes to me at a church potluck
perfumed with frankincense and lasagna.

He believes I am a gentle bird girl
in my tulip sweater and raincoat.

I am not so gentle, but I act as if
and what I act as if I might become.

He says *Let's be still and know refreshments.*
Tater tot casserole is wholesome fare.
Let's get soft, let's get really, really soft.

I do not say *I am frightened of growing plump;*
something about the eye of a needle
and sidling right up close to godliness.

Instead I dig in,
stuff myself on homemade rolls,
chicken pie and cream chipped beef with noodles.

I eat until my bird bones evanesce.
I eat until I bust from my garments.

I become the burping circus lady
with meaty ham hocks and a sow's neck.

Boy says *Let's get soft, even softer.*
We vibrate at the frequency of angel cake.

Our throats fill with ice cream glossolalia.
The eye of the needle grows wider.
There is room at the organ bench.

I play.

PORTRAIT OF MY MOTHER AS A GOLD DUST WOMAN

She was worshipped for her togs, all owls,
black kimono, glass swans, angel belt.

The mascara was her, but corpsy.
She'd put away her knitting.

What a phantasm said the fans.
What a honeyed reality.

They lit flames in her honor
and took an oath to turquoise.

They felt a unity like babies.
They moved their bowels in solitude.

I tried to grab the oil vial off her neck
to totem with or link our navels

but I couldn't reach it.
I didn't need her to spit glitter

I just wanted to plant my crib inside her head
and play with stacking blocks.

The sum of us seemed like a tiny egg.
Maybe it was.

OBITUARY

When I was a boy your age
I lived on a planet called Earth
I think I miss that shitty old time
Nitrate tubing we called *hot dogs*

Put a telescope up to your eye
If from your mouth comes questions
Do you ever? Did you ever?
You'll only write a history book

Marked *deluxe* and *wet*
Though no star is a hot dog
And every galaxy is skippable
Don't let us old farts fool you

But if you put nothing to your eye
Take the questions out of your mouth
I'll let you kiss me on the lips
And suck my ancient oxygen

UMBRELLA POEM

In the coat closet there were 500 umbrellas,

none of them mine.

There was a parasol covered in thistles

I wouldn't touch.

Somebody'd left a company umbrella

Nolan, Armstrong, Curry and Weinstock.

There was a Rolling Rock umbrella

a year of the sheep umbrella

and a plain peach umbrella

(which resembled a peach)

spilling out of the closet door.

How could all of these umbrellas exist?

I wanted to claim a pebble grey umbrella

from Lantern's on the Beach

and parade it around,

be a seafoam solace person

or a moneyed surfer person

or a woman with shell-ensconced breasts

who enjoys oysters Rockefeller

and baked stuffed lobster.

Somebody whole please.

Somebody who looks whole.

SUPERDOOM

There are 200 flavors of panic,
the worst is seeing with no eyes.
Cowboys call it riding your feelings.
I call it SUPERDOOM.
On April 5th I was 98% alive.
I saw my blood sugar at the mall
and spilled into a hall of numb light.
The earth kept coming and coming.
Every human was a baby
puncturing my vehicle.
I tried to stuff a TV
in the hole where prayer grows.
A salesman prescribed zen.
I said *How long have you been alive?*
He said *Six minutes.*

SUCH BEAUTIFUL CLOTHES

I mark you into quadrants & hopscotch across

when I reach the edge   I fall off

At the party in the vessel   we have mood

I am projecting a matrix   all over your trousers

but it's real.
                Whose bones are whose?

You maybe know godhead   your skull

is so porous.
              Please take out your interior

& put it in the closet   If you vomit

on the coverlet   I'll look for my jaw.

LEAH

I ran out of Canaan

      and fell
      on unicorn farm

            moss held me still
            they gave me a mare

a quiet Arabian

              I was not forced to ride
     just brush

brushing I went
           into my forehead
    crystals

           grew over my nightgown
           my feet slept
I could hear

           Jacob call me home

rot on that geography
so I stayed

      make no mistake
  a saint

     would saddle up
       and fly over the olive trees

     she can have that
   nosebleed for me

I am staying
inside

      powdered by silence

I do not
puzzle the flow

    I know what I know

     there is a light

there was a coat

BINGE EATING IN 2067

Wild Man is just like me
starved into fractions.

We all are, the whole colony
raised on motherboards

sugar cane screenshots
pixelated onions.

But I have a jaw that seeks chunks
and he has the heart of a fat man.

In his cave we drink vapor ale
snarf dust fowl, sediment meats.

Nothing is enough
he chains me to the rocks

then slaps my growling stomach
until I spew static

making space for ash fish
and elemental octopi.

I find a thighbone in the stone
and think of friends gone missing.

I hear my human heart beat.
I wonder why he has utensils.

When he cooks a real live cassoulet
flesh and fat, no hoax,

I turn my face from the bowl
and put my fingers in his mouth.

GINGER

I fleshed and fleshed on the skewers of sailors.
I kept busting onto their boats
in search of flame.

Was I an egoless starfish?
No, my needs, my needs
have always been needy.

I must have had deafness.
I could not hear my coconut phone
not ringing.

I used my mouth on them too often
and I cracked
or was cracked.

Now I stay away.
I have cabana wits.
I am a pool pearl, no waves.

I find the piggy
in my heart
and barbecue a Hawaiian feast.

I gather heat
from my skin.
I call the heat Professor.

FLORA

When he found her in the closet
purring to tunics about sublime wine
he called a trial-and-errorist
who prescribed a flower cure
at the temple on the hilltop.
Palliative scrolls said *Let lemon trees,*
let orange blossoms, let tulips and let go.
Bleeding cups were added to the mix.
The slave girls in the bougainvillea garden
could not shut down her shaking.
They brewed anemones in a tureen
and dunked her breasts and ass.
They beat her with stems
and promised a new map.
She said *If I cannot slow time*
I will refuse memory.
The slave girls wished to choke her.
They began walking backwards
plucking cherries from trees for insertion.
They buried her mirror in violets
but was it about that?
The temple filled with smells of rot.
The temple filled with smells of sweet.
Overhead, Venus reclined in paint.

AHOY!

By the gates of the walled lung
we stand circled in the dark.

We've come through his throat
by ship.

I say *What if he hiccups?*

I am channeling my grandmom's fears
of common colds and foreign air.
The women judge me silly.

They say *Unsisterly!*
Your angst is old, so old.

To prove myself fierce
I run down the danger corridor
of his guts to his intestines.

There are cabbages and acid.
There are meat screams
and a fancy market.

I am relieved to discover
my favorite gourmet yogurt
with full nutrition labeling.

Indulging in a blueberry variety
on the banks of his duodenum
I watch the villi sway.

It's a scene nearing Monet's *La Riviere*
but I am not a visual person.

My mind is full of letters.

I say *Help me be a sister.*
I mean to say *Don't make me die alone.*

Back at the lung
roommates have been chosen.

TWO

LONESOME COWGIRL

As long as I lived with god in my cupboard
I thought I was living with god;
My eyes never caught on a whiskey glass,
I didn't leave him for an hombre with a Cadillac.
I was doing the deal, my actions arrows,
faith muscles greased.

Somewhere I stopped looking for magic,
sparks in the canyon loam that open like keys.
Pretend to live on the surface a while
and you become a surface dweller.
Once I was a nightrider with a wild rag.
Now I haven't seen a horse in three years.

MIKVEH

Monthly I must snort the universe

   or seduce a hummingbird

betrothed to a ladybird

acclaimed for her art

   a sculptor with clay on her pants

(ugly pants)

don't you understand

   I will not go to god

for milk again.

   Wreck your nest

turn red

make me goddamn seafood soup, bird

   cook intimately with clams

on counter and blood on wall

spoon me up

    that ocean broth

I must be rid of this medusa feeling

    or else

feel my forehead

say *not so scarlet*

    not so evil

and flannel nightclothes

will grow backwards

    over my arms

an arm-based piety.

CIAO MANHATTAN

All day long my skull
That horsey gulper

Goes braying after sherbets
Busts up ventricles

Trashes valves
But pauses somehow

Hinge open
The day falls off its reins

My brassiere goes unhooked
God walks in

And says *I'm back baby*
What now?

We smile at each other
Go horseless and headless

It is so god
When the voice is like wheat

Spooned wheat
In whole milk

Come closer it says
You cute little fucker

Good old god
What a hoofer

Ran around with Edie Sedgwick
Underneath her leopard skin coat

She said *I love you god*
God said *I love you Edie*

And she ate that wheat
In whole milk

Went smokeless and ginless
It was a dazzling year

Then she turned to wheat
I want to turn to wheat

Relieve me of my teeth
God loves my hair.

DE FOREST STATION

She was built with forest brain
so she would learn to say
I know nothing about forests.

It is the geniusest thing
a treehead girl can say
this I know nothing.

She tried to be a DDTberry.
She tried killsyrups.

She did not think another
treehead girl would ever come
but here they are
with matching forests.

Now there are two.
A map might be made.

Come canopy you
DDTberry killsyrup treeheads.
Let's action the kind word
tongue to tree.

Let us fertilize
root and branch.

Let us make map us
and learn to say *help me.*

Help me help me help me
until we go fallow
clean to our unearthliness.

Let us say *help me*
until the cackle crows are stilled.

Help me help me help me.
help me help me help me.

It is the heroist thing
a treehead girl can say.

FLURRY

Snow tonight, brain
of a frightened rabbit
and heart shaped
like a donut.
Feels I'll never know
quiet again. Walk me
to a room on high alert
and bring friends.
There is a chance
we could ripple
hushful; something
about the sum of us
works best.

WATERFALL

The most romantic thing a human being can say
to another human being is *Let me help you vomit.*
No human being has ever said this to me
and I keep going to god too clean as though god
is frightened of muddy feet. If I am missing
a hairpin I don't go at all. Please describe
your vomiting; it is like a psalm to me
a place where wilderness might be new.
Other people's dirt makes a lovely frock.
Grant I be forgiven in the gush.

MEGACHURCH

The altar boys want me
Swooning drunk
They say *If you feel like nonsense*
Get nonsenser
If you feel bananas
Make a sundae already

Oh I do
I want holiness to meet me halfway
Meet me easy
Like a tugboat on glitter water
Hotel music
Ultragloss

So easy to fall in the water
How easy these altar boys come on
Bodies of soap
With pinwheel erections
They eat hamburgers effortlessly
Only some have hips

It is movie night
In their church in America
A crucifixion movie
No a movie about love
They offer me megaCokes
With rum

Rum will make the movie
More romantic
I cannot say
I am undrunk
How I got to be undrunk
Not here

Boredom is going to get crucified here
The whole church is beeping
Glitter water
Glitter rum
Even my nail polish
Beeping.

MERCY

Yesterday the worship rattled like an engine
I said *Let this voltage last forever*
But today is full of soup odor
The pillow drone is loud today

You give me back my light legs
Let us play galaxy spy
Today is such a nothing nothing
Such a supper of prosthetics

I want to buzz all night
I want the full orbit workup
Your power is none of my business
Maybe your hum could just fall from my lips

PUFF

Good sick orbits
on the avenue

Dib and dab
in Pakistani parlor

Parachute bombita
shooting dream gun

Cactus head
and cherry Leb in bottles

Himalayan cream
over piano

Gypsy strings on wild cat
under milk stars

Morrocan honey blooms
from paper into purr

Wouldn't be none left
if we were there.

MAMALA

We need more retired jezebels like Mamala.
A floozy with a heart of gold is as titian
as her rouge, but Mamala's wound is soldered now.
She unwenched herself.

When Mamala went vestal the peppermint wires
of 1000 moustaches frowned, cigars of Cuba
unlit themselves, a cowboy in Texarkana
ceased sweat forever.

It was a terrible year for the garter market
but Mamala had blood on her legs, Mamala's teeth
were on the headboard, Mamala had to do what's right
for Mamala.

You must eat Mamala's heart pastrami and grow fat
inside her beaded apartment. She will speak of she
in third person and you will feel a love like ketchup.
Please model her please.

There appears a hinge in every young woman's life
when ponies fly out of her soul, her tongue catches fire,
a wet corsage falls from the ceiling. Your ponytail
will not protect you.

Mamala will protect you, Mamala will be there
with a licorice muzzle and bridle on your tongue
and she will sing every harlot aria for you
in the key of you.

STEAK NIGHT

    In husbandland I am made
of hamburger, eggs and potatoes

    a food brew really
scraps spackled.

    A kitchen swells around
full of cakes and clocks

    and babydolls not like ham.
        A hash has happened

        the husband is absent
        my marriage dress hangs

        by the stove.
    I put me in my mouth

    to taste patty melts
stripey fats and underblood

    juicy dregs for geraniums.
I could let drops

and grow victory gardens.
Might I cleave a piece to suck?

O the eggs are growing old
or else they're growing lungs.

PRAYER OF THE RESTLESS CARETAKER

May I be present for fleshman.
May I deliver aspirin, oxygen, and fever
for his fever body beeping with the clock.

Make my tongue for sweat wipe,
storytell, my running shoes for rocks.

Shake me in time with his shaking
and grow brain moss, my self
a thermometer
in sick bowl buttermilk.

O docile me, docile!
Mask my frontal lobe
or whichever lobe
is the lobe of bite and want.

Help me to watch television,
then melt me into epsom
and pour me over him like dirt.

ARSON WIFE

If I wanted to burn the house down
I'd axe trees, hoard tires, wield turpentine.

Instead I'll stuff a pair of nude stockings
with old sheitel hairs and strike a match.

I only want you to dance
on my smoking undergarments.

With god's help the pile will reignite
each time you reach the door

so I can pinch a moment alone
beneath my iron skirt.

It's been 5000 days since I first bathed
in Zaydeh's village cottage

but I can lift my latch
and dive inside a milk lagoon

ceilingless save for the mantle of hours.
When you poke with crag fingers

do you believe I hear bells?
Petseleh, I do it to myself.

JACOB'S LADDER

I know everything   about humans   and your planet
help me forget   what I know   come to me
in bliss   or come swollen   just come
the world is bundled   so   you would think
no you should   not think   every thought
has seven arms   use the elbows.

RINGO

When the final Beatle dies
the president hits a kill switch
and all of our possessions
drift like eyelashes
through a crack in the sky.

Mr. Provenzano delights
to see his old Ford Thunderbird
en route to heaven.

Our nerves are oddly oiled
no one cries over vanished dimes
or even paper currency.

We lie in dirt; stray cats by fire.

It's there, ungloved among roots
of ruined rosebushes,
that I invent the knife.

EGO DEATHS OF A QUEEN

I am a maniac
about tendrils.

I powder my wig
to shut up my brain.

I gargle with gold
for kisses

and air kisses.
I cannot say

what changes.
Change comes sitting.

It creeps slow
like fingers.

How good to sit
and spy on yourself.

That's the way
magick works.

Change comes talking.
It is humans

who help me best.
I plant my scepter

behind their eyes.
When they laugh

I vault in.
No king dies.

You would notice
a king dying.

You would cry
like a statue.

I do not cry
I only weep.

I weep to rule the earth.
I want to rule it

like a saucer pig.
I want to rule it

like a jar of blondes.
I want to rule it

with the thing
atop my neck.

But every night
I lose a head.

EARLY 90s PRAYER

From now on let me be a better friend
to the living. How does this pertain
to Kiefer Sutherland? A lot.

When Kiefer goes *Flatline*, the ghost
of bullied Billy Mahoney unghosts
revealing even poltergeist

were tiny hurt people once too. Grant me
rabbit ears for others. Roast me
and ungrandiose me. Let me not pray

for a spirit horse to take me down easy
in a rough draft like Lou Diamond Phillips
as Chavez *y* Chavez. I need not be

the surest shot on Earth. Fling far
Young Guns dream. No more
Billy the Kid for me.

HOW TO UNLINE A JOURNAL

There is a reference to what's left out
only occasionally. Can we identify

page 29 gussied up a little less?
A sense of flux is not conveyed by

Give it a title. A sense of flux is
(not) conveyed by *Died of X.*

Then there's the level of myth,
a going to Hades thing.

I will be more interested in this process.
I see the motion, I give back

an echo chamber. Don't settle
for capturing beautiful things

about that difficulty.
Why would it be anywhere?

BLUE PERIOD

I know
I am menaced
by art.

Underwater
in the Fountain of Neptune
I blew big bubbles

and would have dissolved
into puddles of no-control
if a hand didn't grab my braid.

Call no journey a success
until both intestines
are clear of the Tuscan stone.

I found no nirvana
but impaled on *Rape of the Sabines*
my body went shadowless.

Protect me from museums
if only for the caramel corn
on Pleasure Island.

Drop this carcass on a carousel
in golden age Atlantic City
where the ponies spring.

Once I ate lead paint off a Caravaggio
down to the Cremnitz white.
I felt it needed to breathe.

RAISE YOUR HAND IF YOU'RE SURE

I want to be a child of happy illusion
not sad illusion or truth. All the vehicles
I've used to make the road stop rippling
stopped working. I bought a blue bicycle
with a shovel on back. Nothing stayed buried.
I'm told to sit and watch the road until
a light shines on my condition. That asylum
seems so broken I can't find the sitting.
I don't feel like a tree in the rain.
I feel like an old grocery trading
in fear. I want medicine quick,
the unity that so terrifies me
to begin a strong new cycle
and everybody scared
of feeling can
come spin.

CONCENTRATE

Take comfort in the ocean until it stops working.
Take comfort in your breathing until you stop working.
Don't know why humans cannot stop what they cannot stop.
Set watches ahead.

On my seaglass legs, a refusal to get in bed
and cozy. What is the sex of the child that my teeth
cannot name? Black seaweed on my heart if my belly
ever does go gut.

You can see the borderlandia of cozy life
in splashes on the sink. Foam soap, mucous membrane,
soft water eroding the purest devotion
to discomforting.

If you get too comfortable, turn Lady Poseidon,
an aqueous heart will erase your shape. Look for them
around town, the washed women, every crevice slurred
and peaceful as bream.

FACSIMILE

How have you genitals?
It is enough
you have hands. Copy

your hands. Send them.
Triplicate, I'll open
my throat. I could

make your golem
from meat. The neighbors
will squirt and spy

to see me on the loaf.
Too few fingers. So much
cream. I need kneepads

just to put on lipstick.
This is how skin cripples
in liquid. Slick slots.

I am your widow. You
are alive. Stop writing
poltergeist. Write bodies.

GOOD HOUSEKEEPING

Red was coming through the walls.
Red dribbled on the carpet.
The damask used to be black.
I asked Kate if she'd gotten
her menses on the carpet.
She was sick of my attitude.
Her friend Audre would come over
to tell me I was awful.
They'd revoke my Sappho card.
Save it, sister, save it
for Susan B. Anthony.
She'll be the judge of menses.
She'll be the judge of carpets.

Served me right about the house.
It was done in mother's style.
Now it was a Jell-O mold
cherry with floating fruit.
I couldn't make anything float.
I couldn't make anything boil.
I'd been seeing boys on the sly
but only to test them with forks,
never to coagulate.
Was it all my undoing?
How awful I thought I was.
It dribbled on the carpet,
it was coming through the walls.

NITROUS OXIDE

My girls are wired for slow death.
Every feather of my girls
wants to moor in more.

Our barstools stand abandoned
on the planet's edge.
Still dogs do push-ups.

At the dentist we cannot
be too prepared.
Seven years since we last pressed

a pedal, sighing *Gas*.
But Loner Harbor takes fast;
don't linger there while he scrapes.

GOLD LIPSTICK AND THE END OF SUMMER

Who knows what old ladies are?

They want their drafts back

Some cannot recall past lives

This must be satisfying

I must be lazy

I can barely grow old

I am hiding in the dollhouse

All my girls are there

Aloha girls

Road-stained warrior trucking girls

Ski holiday village girls

Girls with forks of fat

Saintly girls on rosary hum

Disco marigolds

Gingerbread goodie-goodies

Little punk rabbits.

THREE

LAISSEZ FANFIC

Diaries are for heaven. You know zilch
about growing things. Let your hero grow
himself. Let him eat chard. He will find
his own verbs and find you in the rain.
He will say *Let me extricate you, baby,
from your cronies.* You have no cronies.
Keep mum. This is a hero who knows fungus
from lavender. Let him do the saving.
You don't need a seascape, you don't
even need a setting. Be a bowl
of tangerines. Be no thing.

FUGAZI SHAME

No Fugazi trains ever ran for little old me
the Pink Floyd shuttle provided alternate service
between duckling and chicken. I feel passed over, I'm
a pity pot, I

cannot blame my parents no punk boyfriend delivered
the perfect mixtapes; I was too busy waiting
for cashout at King Soopers, sick to death of slicing
choice boneless ribeye

or otherwise engaged at the *Dark Side of the Moon*
laser light show, 27 times, holding Chronic
in a Barbie lunchbox (I preferred to be the one
holding, I really

love power). Yes, sometimes it seems everybody
good got a piece of Ian McKaye growing up, girls
even; at a book shop in Littleton, one lady
told me she listened

to Christian rock exclusively before she landed
Ian; Fugazi about-faced her from *a dunghole-
snarfing-piggie, a spectator, security guard
for a shit shelter*

to a baby blanket of perfect compassion.
Fugazi is an American punk band formed
in 1987. I never got to be
a fallen Christian.

SEVENTH GRADE LIGHT BRIGADE

I wished Lisa dead Lisa & her wonder world
Lisa and her makeup team but I suppose I didn't
want to watch her die because when she choked
on a giant smartphone I called out *Lisa Lisa
can you talk can you cough can you sing?* & pounded
between her shoulder blades with three sharp blows
which failed to dislodge the giant smartphone
& Lisa fell down ringing reaching with taupe nails
for my unpolished toes so I suppose I imagined
it was me falling backwards through softball practice
& family dinners a turkey drumstick
all turning to glitter when from some magic well
I pulled a starlet Heimlich maneuver
until her voicemail gurgle became a steady breath
& her instant messenger a tumultuous cough
& her highlights sparkled as she burst into song
& the texting halted & the vibrating stopped.

LACK

I found the Summer of Love in a trash can at Hardee's & I ate it.
I found it snaked under a gluten-sensitive thickburger,

a big hot ham 'n cheese & a side salad. You want revolution?
That's another trip. I only know what it feels like to eat

the Summer of Love & what it feels like for this body, a body
lashed by machines. I have two desk machines, a lap machine

& a talk machine. I have a hair machine & a sex machine.
I have a machine for acting as if, a machine for duck & run

& a machine to knock your socks off. I have always cherished
my machines & I have always cherished not thinking

about anybody other than my body, but ever since I ate
the Summer of Love I have not stopped dreaming of babies.

GATE 27

The flight to Miami was delayed three hours
and I was in black. Customer service
ate Burger King French fries, applied
Nivea hand cream. It's easy

to get irate. Could god smell my fake tan
when I heard *There's a 6:55*
to Ft. Lauderdale. Take it. The traveler
in front was a white boy with dreads

and a wooden earring. I offered him
a granola bar if he'd let me cut.
I asked if his boots were vegan. He said
No, they're boots of Spanish leather.

He said *Customer service*
is a capitalist microcosm.
He said *Kurt Cobain died*
at the same age as Jim Morrison.

At 18 I said those things too.
Through words, little gods pop up,
even in the late-teenage sections.
Isn't that the way we remember history?

I just want to go part by part. I don't think
there is a pattern to be found, but I like
the method of constructing tent poles
and refashioning fabric around them.

It's very important to me
that there be a sense of unity.

30TH EDITION

When I remake Lolita
with my old English teacher

I'm not enough
gangly bones.

      The rule is

he must burrow in my convex

      while I coldly
      call him fruithead.

           An extra milk molecule
           tips.

Somebody forgot to freeze me.

Nymphets don't vibrate
in their bobby socks.

      I am supposed to be cork dry.
      I am a fat fish.

        Nevermind a dolly

when I'm legal to buy weaponry.

    If a jury doesn't care
    what I do with my torso

then call me Humbert.

SHARON TATE, MAN UP

I speak for all of us Sharon Tate
when I tell you I eat my toenails

for breakfast, Monkee Mickey Dolenz
never looked at me twice Sharon Tate

you Saint Laurent lipstick Sharon Tate
you python heels and zebra skin bag

Sharon Tate, you wanna know crazy
Sharon Tate? I got the blues and you

got the USA, I got girl dirt
and you're a Seconal marigold;

Warren Beatty never winked at me
you vodka tonic snowflake tittied

Tate, you praise my skeleton Sharon
I speak for all of us when I say

I like the taste of scabs, Steve McQueen
never creamed over me Sharon Tate,

you Malibu Barbie, you happy
ending-Nembutal in the Chateau

Marmont barroom, you Paramount
screen test, your footsteps on the moon.

WHEN ENVY WENT TO DIE

I could not believe what a cinnamon feeling
this starlet gave me.   I was not dwarved
                  nor rendered mammoth.
I felt like a whole dot   a good dot.

It was as if somebody twirled heather ribbon
over my frontal lobe.
                  Now I could just sit back
and eat corned beef   for the rest of my life.
            Her beauty was a spoon in space.
                        Feed me, I said.

I kept waiting for a monkey inside my brain
to bring me down
            but this was not amphetamine
         and no shadow thoughts befell me.

I mean it when I say love entered
                        through my eyes
Lift mine eyes   & keep lifting mine eyes.

She was the wild opus of a starlet machinist.
            I am proud of our being.
Sometimes it goes light inside late.   I say
congratulations!

DRIVE-IN

We've all been miscast   do you know
    who put us in this crazy film?

Until the end, we say.   *I thought it
    such an awful script until the end.*

    We could forget we were born
but our mothers are streaked
        into our hearts.

    It's like some other mother
tossed our magic glasses to the dahlias.

Let's show up for this thing   anyhow
in color.

    Blessed is the celluloid species
    and blessed is the popcorn.

VERTIGO

One minute Hollywood Boulevard
is a rotating field. Repeat
I am to get your knees below your head.

Afternoon hours feel fenceless.
The drugstore soda fountain drains
and all the other starlets are foxier.

You could murder them.

Now imagine a famous ghost
comes to kiss your crescent face.

Let yourself float says the ghost,
*and where there was only sidewalk
appears a constellation of stars.*

Up above the globe you ask.
In it he says, twirling his moustache.

Watch a starlet on TV. Her lipstick
smells like almonds, flaking off your lips.

See yourself scream in a shower scene.
Eat bloody hamburgers. It's a slasher.

You always wanted a witness
to lift you from the crowd.
Now you don't even need jewelry.

Watch your bracelets dissolve like tablets.
The Hollywood sign tumbles in your soup
and you gobble up the alphabet.

You are the breeze rolling down Topanga.

At sunset watch the ghost go poof
but you are him too. Watch grass glow.

AFRICAN PRIESTESS, COLUMBUS CIRCLE

She said: Do you believe in anything?
I said: I weigh my food.
I said: I cried for an hors d'hoeuvre.
I said: I gave away Gramma's pizzelles

to a crackhead at Penn Station.
She said: There's no crackheads at Penn Station.
I said: They were made with eggs.
I said: I hoped the eggs would cure him.

She said: You're killing the wrong person.
I said: His eyes were like cherry clafouti.
She said: I don't care how you slice a cake.
She said: It's still a cake.

I said: Flourless flour noted.
She said: You violate the goddess.
I said: Butterless butter noted.
She said: Your ass is grass.

I said: Creamless creamer noted.
I said: Sugarless sugar noted.
I said: Maybe I'm lonely.
She said: Bingo baby!

HARRIET

I lost a bunny in the wall
where other animalia dwell

a jackal, a panther, a thunderbird.

The bunny would be shish kebab by nightfall
unless I lured it out with apricots
or juicy plums, which I did not have.

I had my voice.

I was like *goddamnit!*
Is your name Happy or Penelope?
Diamond Jim or Harriet?

The naming of that bun
broke a yolk on the moon

but I do not know another way
to call a creature home.

HYDROPONICS

He said *drop your notebook
the temple is everywhere.*

He said a magic mushroom
would eliminate tennis nose
and lend feather atmosphere.

We dropped the drop.
Chimney memory
oceaned away.

I felt like a holiday pumpkin.
We were very sweater
holding thicket vigil
until plants curled.

In a different version
we remained in the rift
between breath and vision
and we're still under that flap.

In this version we exited
to confront a restaurant.
I got touchy
about ranch dressing.

He knew how to take a staircase
from stem to lesson.

I made it about object itself:
stem and mushroom.

I couldn't stop
collecting spores.

I was shoehorning
stamens into a container
trying to architect
the whole diorama.

My arms were like cupboards.
I wouldn't let go of the pipe.

He pointed to the staircase
and I said *ethanol*.

I put him in a locker
and entered the grain range.

It was cannibal tundra.
I was conductor.

My eye was a centimeter
but I never drank
a pink girl drink.

BYE

When I die I regret the dieting
and literary theory. I am just
oh my god one raspberry left. Strange
how we had different experiences.
I would love to have handed you toilet paper
under a stall door. I was thinking with my head
and forgot about my hands. I also regret
the obsessing over ragged seams.
Funny thing is: sometimes the obsessing
called attention to itself doing it
while it did it. I guess we could have gone
naked. Do you know the story of Helen?

TODAY I WILL BE A BENEVOLENT NARRATOR

My little paper people
I am going to love you

Though I do not yet love myself
I ask god for help

I say god, you old stuffed potato
These characters need a yellow kitchen

These characters need a hot dinner
Help me help them

Pull my strings
And I'll even join them at the table

Maybe you will join us too?
Someone else

Can pull your strings
You are tired

You must be so tired
Let's be happy peasants together.

H1N1

Back from the flu today
so in love with power.

I wore a paper nightie
over crinoline slippers

ghost nuns soaped my surfaces
and grunted

*we wish you could see
how not awful you are*

dear sisters devoted only
to helping me vomit

prayer candles
on an avalanche level

I forgot my dialect
of defects entirely

a furry creature
carcassed at the altar

I felt so righteous
I humped a humidifier

climaxed on the linens
dropped dead in tongues

a guilty future chimed
but my tea read *stay*

be not a saint
be queasy

confessing nothing
to a slice of honeyed toast

I was so touched
what I heard myself say.

MR. BUBBLE

I controlled my words, my deeds and nothing more.
God wanted no revenge on my body.

I was afraid to do good will for my body
or I might vanish. I was a child and you were too.

Let us bathe each other and exact revenge.
Everybody needs a lot of fathers.

When I am father I will sew us curtains
made of other men's voices, first a patch then a moan.

Sometimes the curtains will come between us.
Mostly they will be around us.

When you are father you will build me a hardhat
with a light in it. I will not be afraid of light.

I will feel my muscles under me
like good pavement. Beauty won't kill me in the street.

Then will come a silence over every house
and every town, a year of it but up.

In the air among the insects, our first bodies
and everything we don't know about physics.

PINK KEDS

Girls are building a tower
of love shoes
          on your neighbor's doorstep
     pink Keds
            uncasual flats
deer moccasins
Tone 'n' Go's
            silver d'Orsays
    gardening clogs
demiboots
sensible sandals

        consider the options
what are the options?

        bone-bruising babes
    ballerina buttocks

melon bellies
    breath of fruit

        palatial navels
    ankle thorns
           cloudburst nipples

    wolf pie supper

NO HOSTAGES

Head life is a dangerous neighborhood.
It's a jungle in here.
        My eyebrows house a bullet.
        Somebody planted a hive
at birth.

    The doctors weighed my cranium.
            They didn't count
adrenaline.   They said 6 *ounces*.
That was their end.

        They left me dreaming
it was autumn.   I sang an acid anthem.
I would do anything
        to get out of here.
    I will still do almost anything.

I could say   *Let's light up everything.*
We could hump the sun all day.
    I crave tremors in this skull room.
I crave the good kind.

        Set me on fire!
Send happy mail and pastries.   Send
drama drama drama.
    We could go manic on charm.

      We could make us sweethearts easy.
                The sweethearts part
is easy.   It takes guts
to just sit here.   I am just
going to sit here.

BEACH HOUSE

She shook her parcel of babies
Showed the landscape of her womb
Gardens starred with dahlias
Acacias dripping minerals
Over a carefully cloistered sea

She cried out for me
To quit her bridegroom
Sipping at my nipples
He called them pompoms
Lava lamps

A cake of soap exploded
I'd apocalypsed
His corn flakes
His body spelled backwards
He had to lie still all the time

Things I could not have
I should not want
I wanted
I ran my engine in her garage
The crockery went with me.

MONEY HONEY

The fake gods call to say hello.
They ask that I stop chanting *Levitate me.*
It's not going to happen.

They've got a psychic on loan selling airline peanuts
from 5000 years ago of our good Lord.

The psychic is faux too
but when she feels my wrist for pulse,
all systems flicker.

She says *Face up spacegirl you're lonely.*
You've not been felt in centuries.

She's standing on my chart
holding bum cards.
But she's still got teeth in her head.

I whisper *Hey witch what's for dinner?*
Strawberry candles and peanuts.

We choose wands
to bruise each other purple.
We black out the windows and let tongues glitter.

I eat her magic peanuts, burping soft tarantulas.
I say *Will you please botch my future?*

FAUNA

They called it a meat prayer
blood bubbles to heaven.
We would roast Mr. White
with cherries on a spit
by the ocean.

They promised me
pina colada.

They promised the meal
would suffocate
all memory
until I screamed
dear rabbit god!

But I remember everything
the evening's fabric
lacking candles
no sense of orchid

how I said
I would rather dream
of Jerusalem
than go
to Jerusalem
over his gumbo ribs.

Oh drumless air!
Oh garbage food!

No more feathers
than boiler chicken
no more ascension
than sweetbreads.

I split his lip for figs
and lit a limb
but I am still
carrying my head.

IT IS GOOD

It is good for the sky
to fall down around you

and good for the wrong plants
to grow in your houseplants

strange plants
mushrooms even

but it would be a lie
if I said that the heart

is not made out of meat
a fat and fatal core

where ether is everywhere
and electricity bends

I do not know why
we cannot

make the whole
story up.

ACKNOWLEDGMENTS

Thanks to the editors of the journals in which some of these poems first appeared, sometimes a little differently:

Action, Yes: "30th Edition," "Binge Eating in 2067," "Hydroponics," "Leah," "Obituary"
The Awl: "Megachurch," "Steak Night," "Waterfall"
Barrelhouse: "Arson Wife"
Bluestem: "Bones," "Laissez Fanfic," "Pink Keds"
The Collagist: "H1N1"
Court Green: "Ciao Manhattan," "Mamala"
Drunken Boat: "Gold Lipstick & the End of Summer"
Everyday Genius: "The Mail"
Five Dials: "African Priestess, Columbus Circle"
Guernica: "Championship"
H_NGM_N: "Lonesome Cowgirl"
HTMLGIANT: "Supper"
inter|upture: "Flora," "Flurry"
Lamination Colony: "Good Housekeeping"
Loaded Bicycle: "Harriet," "Meat Heart"
Lo-Ball: "Today I will Be a Benevolent Narrator"
Miracle Monacle: "Gate 27"
The Morning News: "Mikvah"
NOÖ Journal: "Ahoy!"
On Earth As it Is: "Early 90s Prayer," "Pennsylvania Prayer"
PANK: "Bye," "Sharon Tate, Man Up"
Redivider: "Blue Period"

Vinyl: "Fugazi Shame," "Seventh Grade Light Brigade"
Women's Studies Quarterly: "Fauna"
Word / for Word: "How to Unline a Journal"

Thanks to Elaine Equi, David Groff, Natalie Lyalin, Dorothea Lasky, Mark Bibbins, Chris Toll, Dan Lichtenberg, Linda and Robert Broder, Hayley Broder, Margaret Curry, Shoshanna Must, the SHAS girls, Ryan Call, Kristen Iskandrian, the CCNY kids, and Leigh Hovey.

Biggest thanks to the master genius Adam Robinson. You are the best.

Meat of my heart to Nicholas.

Melissa Broder is also the author of the poetry collection *When You Say One Thing but Mean Your Mother*. She lives in Brooklyn.